To my mother, Gerri, for her endless love

JANETTA OTTER-BARRY BOOKS

Eye on the Wild: Orang-utan copyright © Frances Lincoln Limited 2013
Text and photographs copyright © Suzi Eszterhas 2013

The right of Suzi Eszterhas to be identified as the author and photographer of this work
has been asserted by her in accordance with the Copyright, Designs and Patents Act,
1988 (United Kingdom).

First published in Great Britain in 2013 by
Frances Lincoln Children's Books, 4 Torriano Mews,
Torriano Avenue, London NW5 2RZ
www.franceslincoln.com

A catalogue record for this book is available from the British Library.

ISBN 978-1-84780-313-9

Set in Stempel Schneidler

Printed in China by C&C Offset Printing Co., Ltd in November 2012

1 3 5 7 9 8 6 4 2

ORANG-UTAN

Suzi Eszterhas

F

FRANCES LINCOLN
CHILDREN'S BOOKS

High in the trees of the rainforest in Sumatra, a baby orang-utan is born. The tiny baby will spend the first few months of her life snuggled up against her mother's warm chest. She is so weak she can barely raise her head. But her little fingers are very strong and she will use them to cling to her mum's long red fur.

The orang-utan mum holds her baby close, to keep her safe and warm in the wet jungle. She loves her baby very much and gives her lots of hugs and kisses. Like human babies, orang-utan babies stay with their mums for a long time. For six years the baby orang-utan will watch everything her mother does to learn how to live in the forest.

Clinging to her mother, the orang-utan baby is always close to her milk. Mum's milk is like a drinking fountain and the baby can even drink while Mum is climbing. She is always hungry and needs to drink lots of milk to grow big and strong.

Orang-utans spend most of the time
in the trees of their rainforest home.
For an orang-utan, travelling through the trees
is fast and easy. Mum is like an acrobat and
uses her long arms to swing from branch
to branch. Sometimes they are really high up,
so the baby has to hold on very tightly.

Mum climbs high in the trees to look for fruit and leaves to eat. When the baby is four months old she is ready to try fruit. Mum teaches her baby where to find the sweetest fruit and the freshest leaves. She mashes up the fruit with her teeth and then gives it to the baby to taste.

On the baby orang-utan's first birthday climbing lessons begin. The baby loves to climb but it takes a lot of practice. Sometimes she gets dizzy but Mum is always close by, ready to catch her if she falls. One day, when she grows up, she will be an expert climber like her mum.

All that climbing is hard work and it's time for a rest. Mum bends branches down to make a comfortable bed of leaves and twigs to relax in. This is called a nest. Mum is sleepy and hoping to take a nap, but the baby is bursting with energy and wants to keep climbing. Mum is careful to hold her hand to make sure she doesn't fall from the nest.

The orang-utan baby loves to play, and so does Mum. The forest is like a huge playground and they have loads of fun swinging and jumping around. But playing isn't just good fun, it will also help the baby grow the strong arms that she needs for climbing.

Sometimes the mother and her baby
come across other orang-utans in the forest.
The baby is a bit shy when meeting others
for the first time, so she clings to Mum's side.
But with Mum's encouragement she begins
to play with her new friend.

When the baby orang-utan gets sleepy, she can take a nap any time. Mum's back is always a cosy place for a snooze. She is getting bigger every day, but she still needs lots of sleep.

When the baby is four years old it is time for some real exploring. Mum shows her around their forest home and is always nearby to lend a hand. They take strolls on the forest floor, climb cliffs and look for treasures, like washed-up fruit beside the river.

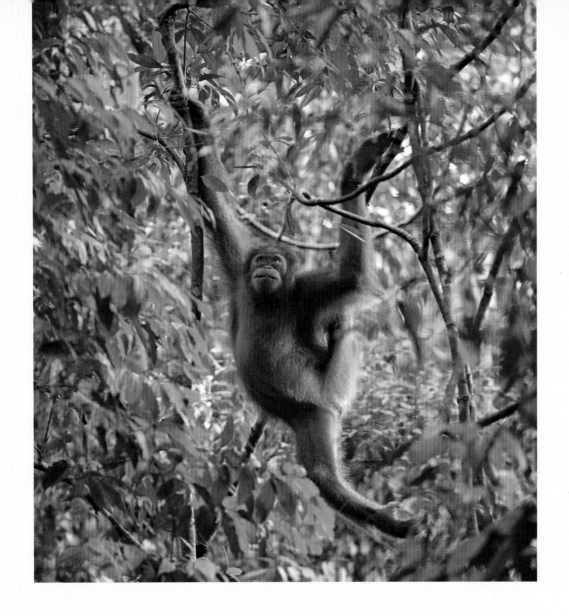

On her fifth birthday the young orang-utan is nearly grown-up. She leaves her mother to have some exciting adventures of her own. It's a bit scary at first without Mum but she remembers all the things Mum has taught her about living in the forest.

The young orang-utan needs to find her own food. Luckily, her mum has taught her well and this is easy. She now knows when and where to look for her favourite fruit and how to find the most delicious leaves. She even finds some yummy bugs in a piece of wood.

She also meets other young orang-utans in the forest. She's a bit lonely without her mum, so she loves to hang out with friends. Sometimes they spend many days together, rolling around and playing, racing each other to the tops of trees, exploring the forest and looking for food.

One day the young orang-utan finds her mum in the forest. They are both very happy to see each other again and spend a few days together. Being with Mum is great, but the young orang-utan needs to start her own family and soon she goes off on her own again. Throughout her life she will often see her mum in the forest.

When the young orang-utan is six years old she is grown-up. One day soon she will have her own little baby clinging to her chest, while she swings through the trees. She will teach her baby the secrets of the forest – how to find food, climb, and stay safe from danger. And one day she will introduce the baby to her mother – Grandma orang-utan.

More about Orang-utans

- Orang-utans live in Indonesia and Malaysia on the islands of Borneo and Sumatra.

- The word orang-utan comes from the Malay language and means 'person of the forest'.

- Orang-utans are very intelligent and are close relatives of humans. We share 96.4% of our genetic make-up with orang-utans.

- Orang-utans use tools. They make umbrellas out of big leaves when it rains, and use sticks to get honey from beehives.

- Orang-utans eat over 300 different foods, including fruit, leaves, flowers, honey, bark, insects and even clay.

- Orang-utans have really long arms. When they stand, their hands nearly touch the ground.

- An orang-utan is seven times stronger than a human.

- Male orang-utans grow a beard and moustache when they become adults. Later in life male orang-utans grow cheek pads and throat pouches.

- A male orang-utan's call is called a 'long call' and it can be heard over a mile or 1.6 kilometres away.

- Orang-utans are endangered because people are cutting down their rainforest homes.

- For more information visit www.orangutans-sos.org